ESCAPE THE ORDINARY

A 30 DAY ADVENTURE WITH NATURE

Aditya Ruhela

"A night under the stars will teach you more than a thousand books ever could."

Contents

Author's Note

Why Nature Matters in today's Fast Paced World?

In a world dominated by screens, deadlines, and constant distractions, we often forget the simple joys of life. The rustling of leaves, the whisper of the wind, and the warmth of the sun on our skin, these are the experiences that ground us, remind us of who we truly are, and reconnect us to the essence of life. Yet, as modern living pulls us deeper into the digital realm, we find ourselves increasingly detached from nature, from adventure, and from the wild spirit that once defined humanity.

This book is an invitation, a call to break free from routine and rediscover the beauty of the outdoors. Whether you're a seasoned adventurer or someone who has never set foot on a trail, this journey is for you. It's about escaping the mundane and stepping into a world of wonder, challenge, and self discovery.

My Personal Journey with Nature & Adventure

My love for nature wasn't something I found overnight. It was a series of small moments, camping under the stars, feeling the thrill of reaching a mountain peak, and experiencing the peace that comes with listening to a flowing river. Each adventure added a new layer to my understanding of life. I realized that nature is not just a place to visit; it is a way of being. It teaches resilience, patience, and the art of truly living.

The 30 Day Nature Challenge is a reflection of this journey. It is designed to guide you through small, yet profound experiences that will transform the way you see the world around you. From the simple act of walking barefoot on grass to the thrill of camping in the wild, each challenge is a step toward reconnecting with the natural world and, ultimately, yourself.

How This Book Will Change Your Life?

This book isn't just about spending time outdoors it's about transformation. Every day, for 30 days, you will be challenged to step out of your comfort zone and engage with nature in a way you never have before. You will slow down, observe, breathe, and truly experience the world around you. And by the end of this journey, you will not only have rediscovered nature but also a part of yourself that may have been long forgotten.

So, are you ready to escape the ordinary? Let's begin.

"Disconnect to truly connect not just with nature, but with yourself."

Introduction

What is the 30 Day Nature Challenge?

The 30 Day Nature Challenge is a carefully designed journey to reconnect you with the outdoors, one simple step at a time. Each day presents a new adventure, a small but meaningful activity that brings you closer to nature and allows you to experience the world in a way you may have never considered before.

This challenge is not about extreme survival skills or pushing yourself to the limits; rather, it's about rediscovering the joy of being outside, appreciating the natural world, and building habits that will stay with you for a lifetime. Whether you live in a bustling city or the countryside, these activities are adaptable to any environment, ensuring that anyone can embark on this journey.

How to Use This Book?

This book is structured to guide you through a progressive journey of nature immersion. The challenges start small like watching a sunrise, walking barefoot on the grass and gradually lead to deeper experiences such as a digital detox, stargazing, and even planning a multi day camping trip.

You can follow the challenge as designed, taking it one day at a time, or adjust it to fit your schedule and lifestyle. The goal is not perfection but participation. Engage with each activity at your own pace, allowing yourself the freedom to explore, learn, and enjoy the process.

Each challenge includes:

- **A brief explanation** of the activity and why it matters.
- **Step by step instructions** to make it easy to follow.
- **Reflections & journaling prompts** to help you document your experience.

At the end of this journey, you will have built a habit of spending time in nature, feeling more connected to the world around you, and developing a deeper appreciation for outdoor adventures.

The Science behind Nature's Impact on Mental and Physical Well being

Numerous studies have shown that spending time in nature has profound benefits for both mental and physical health. Exposure to natural environments has been linked to reduced stress levels, improved mood, increased creativity, and enhanced focus.

Here are just a few scientifically backed reasons why this challenge will positively impact your life:

- **Boosts Mental Health** : Time in nature lowers cortisol levels, reducing stress and anxiety. Studies suggest that even a short walk in a green space can improve mood and concentration.
- **Enhances Physical Health** : Activities like hiking, walking, and even sitting outdoors expose you to fresh air, natural sunlight (which boosts vitamin D), and opportunities for physical exercise.
- **Increases Creativity and Problem Solving Skills** : Disconnecting from screens and engaging with nature has been found to enhance creative thinking and cognitive function.
- **Encourages Mindfulness** : Nature allows us to slow down, be present in the moment, and cultivate a deeper awareness of ourselves and our surroundings.

With this challenge, you will not only experience these benefits first hand but also create lasting habits that will enrich your daily life far beyond these 30 days.

Are you ready to embark on this journey? Let's take the first step

Week 1: Reconnecting with Nature : The First Step

The first week of your **30 day journey** is all about slowing down and rediscovering the simple joys of nature. This phase focuses on awakening your senses, grounding yourself, and building a deeper awareness of the natural world around you.

- You'll begin by witnessing the serene beauty of sunrise, experiencing how the first light of day can bring clarity and peace.
- As you walk barefoot on the earth, you'll learn to connect physically with nature, feeling its textures and energy beneath your feet.
- Through mindful observation, you'll notice the tiny details of the world the patterns of leaves, the songs of birds, the way the wind moves.
- You'll start your own nature journal, a personal space to document thoughts, reflections, and discoveries from your time outdoors.

- Practicing deep breathing in green spaces will help you absorb fresh oxygen while calming your mind.
- A picnic without screens will remind you of the joy of being present, fully engaged with your surroundings and companions.
- Finally, you'll seek true silence, spending a moment alone in nature to reflect, recharge, and embrace the peace that comes with solitude.

By the end of Week 1, you will have slowed down, tuned in, and taken your first steps toward a deeper connection with the natural world. Now, you are ready to step into more adventurous experiences in the coming weeks!

Day 1: Sunrise Therapy : Watching the First Light of the Day

Sunrises symbolize new beginnings, peace, and a fresh perspective on life. Witnessing the first light of the day connects you to nature's rhythm and helps you start with mindfulness and positivity.

How to Do It:

1. **Find the Perfect Spot** : Choose a location with an open view of the horizon. A park, hilltop, beach, or even your balcony can work.
2. **Wake Up Early** : Check the sunrise time in your area and wake up at least 15 minutes before.
3. **Observe in Silence** : As the sky shifts in colour, take deep breaths and simply be present in the moment.
4. **Engage Your Senses** : Listen to the birds, feel the cool morning air, and notice the way light changes around you.
5. **Reflect or Journal** : Write about how this experience made you feel. Did it bring clarity, joy, or a sense of calm?

Why This Matters:

- **Reduces Stress** : Nature's early morning serenity can lower anxiety and improve mood.
- **Boosts Positivity** : Starting the day with a peaceful moment sets a positive tone.
- **Strengthens Connection with Nature** : You become more aware of the natural world's cycles.

Nature Journal Insight:

- *How did watching the sunrise make you feel?*
- *Did this experience change the way you see mornings?*
- *Will you make sunrise therapy a habit in your life?*

Day 2: Walk Barefoot : Grounding Yourself with Nature

Walking barefoot, also known as "earthing," is a simple yet powerful way to connect with nature. It allows you to feel the earth beneath your feet, promoting relaxation, balance, and a sense of being grounded in the present moment.

How to Do It:

1. **Find a Natural Surface** : Choose a soft, safe place like grass, soil, sand, or even smooth rocks.
2. **Remove Your Shoes & Socks** : Let your feet make direct contact with the ground.
3. **Take Slow, Intentional Steps** : Pay attention to how the earth feels cool, warm, soft, or textured.
4. **Breathe Deeply & Absorb the Energy** : Close your eyes for a moment and feel the connection. Imagine the earth's energy flowing into you.
5. **Walk for at Least 10 15 Minutes** : The longer you walk, the more you'll relax and attune to nature's rhythm.

Why This Matters:

- **Improves Circulation** : Stimulates nerve endings and increases blood flow.
- **Reduces Stress & Anxiety** : Helps calm the nervous system and promotes a sense of peace.
- **Strengthens Your Connection to Nature** : Encourages mindfulness and presence.

Nature Journal Insight:

- *How did it feel to walk barefoot?*
- *Did you notice anything different in your surroundings compared to when you wear shoes?*
- *Would you consider making barefoot walks a regular practice?*

Day 3: The Art of Observation : Noticing the Little Details around You

Nature is filled with wonders, but in our fast paced lives, we often overlook the small yet beautiful details around us. Today's challenge is all about slowing down, sharpening your senses, and truly seeing the world with fresh eyes.

How to Do It:

1. **Choose a Spot in Nature** : It could be a park, a garden, a forest trail, or even your backyard.
2. **Sit or Walk Slowly** : Instead of rushing, take your time to notice the environment.
3. **Engage Your Senses** : Look at patterns on leaves, listen to distant bird songs, feel the texture of tree bark, or smell the freshness of the air.
4. **Find something you've Never Noticed Before** : Maybe it's a tiny insect, a unique leaf shape, or the way sunlight filters through the trees.
5. **Sketch or Write about It** : If you have a journal, document what you observed. If you enjoy photography, capture an interesting detail.

Why This Matters:

- **Enhances Mindfulness** : Helps you stay present in the moment.
- **Strengthens Your Connection with Nature** : Deepens appreciation for the small wonders around you.
- **Boosts Creativity & Focus** : Encourages a more curious and observant mind set.

Nature Journal Insight:

- *What new details did you observe today?*
- *Did slowing down change the way you see nature?*
- *How did this experience make you feel?*

Day 4: Create a Nature Journal : Documenting Your Outdoor Experiences

Journaling is a powerful way to deepen your connection with nature. By recording your thoughts, observations, and experiences, you create a personal log of your journey, making each outdoor moment more meaningful and memorable.

How to Do It:

1. **Find a Notebook or Use a Digital Journal** : Choose a format that feels comfortable. A simple notebook, sketchpad, or even a note taking app works well.
2. **Start with Today's Experience** : Reflect on what you saw, heard, or felt during your time outside.
3. **Use Descriptive Writing** : Try to capture the experience vividly. Example: "The breeze carried the scent of pine, and the golden sunlight danced on the leaves."
4. **Add Sketches or Photos** : Draw a leaf, a bird, or a landscape. If you prefer, take pictures and attach them to your journal.
5. **Write Daily or Weekly** : Make journaling a habit to track your growth and experiences throughout the 30 day challenge.

Why This Matters:

- **Deepens Your Connection with Nature** : Writing enhances appreciation and understanding of the environment.
- **Boosts Mindfulness & Reflection** : Helps you slow down and process your thoughts.
- **Creates a Personal Memory Book** : You'll have a beautiful record of your journey to look back on.

Nature Journal Insight:

- *What did you write about today?*
- *Did the act of journaling make you notice more details?*
- *How did putting your thoughts on paper (or screen) make you feel?*

Day 5: Deep Breathing in Green Spaces : Oxygenating Your Mind

In our busy lives, we often forget one of the most fundamental aspects of well being, our breath. Breathing deeply in a natural setting not only calms the mind but also revitalizes the body by filling our lungs with fresh, oxygen rich air. Today's challenge focuses on harnessing the power of breath in nature to boost clarity, relaxation, and overall health.

How to Do It:

1. **Find a Quiet, Green Space** : A park, garden, forest, or even a spot with a few trees will work.
2. **Sit or Stand Comfortably** : Keep your spine straight and shoulders relaxed.
3. **Close Your Eyes & Inhale Deeply** : Breathe in slowly through your nose, filling your lungs completely. Hold for a moment.
4. **Exhale Gently Through Your Mouth** : Release the breath slowly, letting go of any tension.
5. **Repeat for 5 10 Minutes** : Focus only on your breathing, feeling the fresh air rejuvenate your body.
6. **Observe Any Changes** : Notice how your body and mind feel after this practice.

Why This Matters:

- **Reduces Stress & Anxiety** : Deep breathing activates the relaxation response in your body.
- **Improves Oxygen Flow** : Increases energy and mental clarity.
- **Connects you to the Present Moment** : Helps you feel more grounded in nature.

Nature Journal Insight:

- *How did deep breathing in a natural space make you feel?*
- *Did you notice a change in your stress levels or focus?*
- *Will you continue using this technique in daily life?*

Day 6: A Picnic with No Screens : Being Present in the Moment

In today's digital age, it's rare to experience a moment without the presence of screens. We eat meals while scrolling through our phones, listen to music while walking, and check notifications constantly. Today's challenge is about breaking free from this habit by enjoying a picnic without any distractions, just you, your meal, and nature.

How to Do It:

1. **Pick a Scenic Spot** : A park, forest, lakeside, or even your backyard. Anywhere peaceful and surrounded by nature.
2. **Prepare a Simple Meal** : Pack fresh fruits, sandwiches, or anything easy to carry.
3. **Leave Your Phone Behind (or on Airplane Mode)** : Resist the temptation to check messages or social media.
4. **Engage Your Senses** : Notice the sounds, textures, smells, and colours around you. Feel the sun on your skin, listen to birds, and observe the movement of the trees.
5. **Eat Mindfully** : Savour every bite, appreciating the flavours and the moment itself.

6. **Spend at Least 30 Minutes in the Present** : After eating, simply relax. Watch the clouds, journal, or even lie down and soak in the experience.

Why This Matters:

- **Enhances Mindfulness** : Helps you reconnect with the present moment.
- **Reduces Digital Fatigue** : A break from screens refreshes your mind.
- **Strengthens Your Connection with Nature** : Allows for a more immersive experience outdoors.

Nature Journal Insight:

- *How did it feel to disconnect from screens during your meal?*
- *Did you notice anything about nature that you usually overlook?*
- *Will you incorporate more screen free moments into your daily life?*

Day 7: Finding Silence : A Solo Moment with Nature

We live in a world filled with constant noise traffic, notifications, conversations, and background distractions. True silence is a rare gift, but nature offers it freely. Today's challenge is about embracing stillness and solitude, allowing yourself to simply exist in the quiet presence of nature.

How to Do It:

1. **Find a Peaceful Natural Spot** : A secluded park, a forest clearing, a riverside, or even a quiet garden.
2. **Sit Comfortably & Close Your Eyes** : Let go of any expectations and just be.
3. **Listen Without Distraction** : Notice the subtle sounds of the wind, rustling leaves, or distant birdsong.
4. **Breathe Deeply & Slowly** : Absorb the calm energy of nature.
5. **Resist the Urge to Fill the Silence** : No music, no talking, no distractions just stillness.
6. **Stay for At Least 15 30 Minutes** : Observe how your mind and body respond.

Why This Matters:

- **Encourages Inner Peace** : Helps reduce stress and anxiety.
- **Deepens Your Connection with Nature** : Fosters a sense of unity with the environment.
- **Enhances Self Awareness** : Brings clarity and mindfulness into your daily life.

Nature Journal Insight:

- *How did silence feel uncomfortable or peaceful?*
- *Did you notice anything about nature or yourself that you hadn't before?*
- *Will you make time for silent moments in your routine?*

Week 2: Adventure & Exploration : Stepping Outside Your Comfort Zone

In Week 2, you will step beyond your usual routines and embrace adventure. This phase is about exploration, learning new outdoor skills, and deepening your appreciation for nature through hands on experiences.

- You'll begin by exploring a new park or trail, discovering fresh landscapes and expanding your sense of adventure.
- Learning the basics of outdoor navigation will empower you to read maps, use a compass, and find your way without relying on technology.
- As night falls, you'll engage in stargazing, connecting with the vastness of the universe and appreciating the night sky.
- Setting up a small camp in your backyard or a nearby spot will introduce you to the fundamentals of outdoor living.

- You'll experience the joy of cooking outdoors, turning simple ingredients into a meal surrounded by nature's beauty.
- A session of wildlife spotting will help you understand the role animals play in the ecosystem and how to observe them respectfully.
- Finally, you'll take on a nature photography challenge, capturing the beauty of your surroundings and sharpening your ability to notice the little wonders of the wild.

By the end of Week 2, you will have pushed your boundaries, developed new outdoor skills, and deepened your connection with the natural world. The journey continues as we move towards inner peace and mindfulness in the next phase.

Day 8: Exploring a New Park or Trail : Expanding Your Horizons

Nature is vast and full of surprises, but we often stick to familiar places. Today's challenge is about stepping outside your comfort zone and discovering something new whether it's a hidden park in your city, an unfamiliar hiking trail, or a quiet green space you've never explored before.

How to Do It:

1. **Find a New Place** : Look up nearby parks, nature reserves, or trails that you haven't visited before. It could be a well known spot you never explored or a small park in a different part of town.
2. **Go Alone or With a Friend** : Whether you explore solo or with a companion, make sure to be fully present. If you're with someone, encourage quiet observation rather than distractions.
3. **Engage Your Senses** : Notice the different scents, the sounds of birds, the feel of the wind. Compare how this place feels versus the ones you're used to.
4. **Take Notes & Photos** : Write down what stands out. Are the trees different? Do you notice any unique flowers or insects? Take photos, but don't let them distract from the experience.

5. **Reflect on the Journey** : Before leaving, sit quietly for a few moments and absorb the space. How did it feel to be somewhere new?

Why This Matters:

- **Breaks the Routine** : We often get stuck in patterns, and exploring new places helps refresh our minds.
- **Boosts Curiosity** : The more you seek out nature, the more you'll realize how much there is still to discover.
- **Enhances Adaptability** : Being in unfamiliar settings helps build confidence and adaptability.

Nature Journal Insight:

- *What was different about this park or trail compared to your usual spots?*
- *Did you feel a sense of adventure, or was it uncomfortable stepping into a new place?*
- *Would you revisit this place, and why?*

Day 9: Learning the Basics of Outdoor Navigation : Finding Your Way without GPS

In today's digital age, we rely heavily on GPS and smartphones to find our way. But what if you were lost in nature without them? Learning basic navigation skills not only builds confidence but also deepens your connection with the environment.

How to Do It:

1. **Start with a Map & Compass** : If you don't have a compass, download a simple compass app (but avoid using GPS). Try to understand basic directions North, South, East, and West.
2. **Observe Natural Landmarks** : Pay attention to key features around you tall trees, hills, rivers, or unique rocks. Use them as reference points.
3. **Follow the Sun's Position** : In the morning, the sun rises in the east, in the evening, it sets in the west. This can help you determine directions.
4. **Try Navigating a Short Trail without GPS** : If you're in a park or trail, challenge yourself to navigate by memory and natural landmarks rather than using your phone.
5. **Practice Finding Your Way Back** : After walking for a while, pause and try to retrace your steps without looking at any digital aid.

Why This Matters:

- **Builds Self Reliance** : Knowing how to navigate naturally boosts confidence in outdoor adventures.
- **Improves Observation Skills** : You'll start noticing small details in nature that you may have ignored before.
- **Strengthens Survival Skills** : If you ever go deep into the wilderness, basic navigation skills can be lifesaving.

Nature Journal Insight:

- *How did it feel trying to navigate without GPS?*
- *Did you struggle, or did you find it easy?*
- *What was the most helpful technique for you?*

Day 10: Stargazing : Connecting with the Universe

Have you ever looked up at the night sky and felt a sense of wonder? Stargazing reminds us how vast and mysterious the universe is. Tonight, you'll disconnect from daily distractions and immerse yourself in the beauty of the cosmos.

How to Do It:

1. **Find a Dark Spot** : The farther you are from city lights, the better. A rooftop, backyard, or open field works well. If you can, visit a place with minimal light pollution.

2. **Give Your Eyes Time to Adjust** : It takes about 20 minutes for your eyes to fully adjust to darkness. Avoid looking at your phone to keep your night vision sharp.

3. **Look for Constellations** : Try identifying major constellations like Orion, Ursa Major, or the Pleiades. You can use a stargazing app, but try spotting them with your eyes first.

4. **Observe Planets & the Moon** : If the moon is visible, take note of its phase. If you have binoculars, use them to see craters more clearly.

5. **Contemplate the Universe** : Lie down, breathe deeply, and let your mind wander. Think about the vastness of space, the stars that have existed

for millions of years, and your place in the universe.

Why This Matters:

- **Encourages Mindfulness** : Looking at the night sky helps you slow down and be present.
- **Boosts Curiosity** : It sparks interest in astronomy and the mysteries of space.
- **Puts Life in Perspective** : The universe is vast, and our daily worries seem smaller when compared to its immensity.

Nature Journal Insight:

- *How did you feel while looking at the stars?*
- *Did you recognize any constellations?*
- *Did this experience shift your perspective on life in any way?*

Day 11: Setting Up a Small Camp in Your Backyard or Nearby Spot

Camping is one of the best ways to reconnect with nature, but you don't need to travel far to experience it. A simple setup in your backyard, terrace, or a nearby green space can give you a taste of outdoor adventure while teaching essential survival skills.

How to Do It:

1. **Choose Your Spot** : Find a suitable area where you can safely set up camp. It could be your backyard, a terrace, or a nearby park (if allowed).
2. **Set Up a Shelter** : If you have a tent, practice pitching it. If not, create a simple setup with a blanket and a couple of poles or chairs.
3. **Create a Cosy Outdoor Setup** : Bring a sleeping bag, mat, or just a few cushions and blankets to make it comfortable.
4. **Unplug & Immerse Yourself in Nature** : Keep electronic distractions to a minimum. Instead, listen to the night sounds, feel the fresh air, and enjoy the solitude.
5. **Light a Campfire or Use Lanterns** : If it's safe and permitted, make a small fire or use lanterns to create a warm outdoor atmosphere.

6. **Spend the Night or at Least a Few Hours** : If you're comfortable, try sleeping outside. If not, just spend an evening under the open sky.

Why This Matters:

- **Builds Outdoor Skills** : Even a simple camping experience prepares you for future outdoor adventures.
- **Strengthens Resilience & Independence** : Learning to set up a camp boosts confidence and problem solving abilities.
- **Encourages Disconnection & Reflection** : Being in a natural setting helps clear the mind and reduce stress.

Nature Journal Insight:

- *How did it feel to sleep or spend time outside?*
- *What challenges did you face in setting up your shelter?*
- *Did this experience make you more interested in camping?*

Day 12: Cooking Outdoors : A Taste of Adventure

Cooking outdoors is not just about preparing food, it's about engaging your senses, embracing simplicity, and savouring the joy of eating in the open air. Whether you're using a small campfire, a portable stove, or just a simple grill, today's challenge is all about experiencing the magic of outdoor cooking.

How to Do It:

1. **Choose a Simple Outdoor Recipe** : Go for easy to make meals like roasted veggies, grilled sandwiches, boiled potatoes, or a one pot meal.
2. **Set Up a Cooking Spot** : If possible, cook on a small campfire, a portable stove, or even a makeshift grill. If you don't have access to these, a simple picnic setup with ready made ingredients works too.
3. **Use Natural Elements When Possible** : Try using leaves, wooden sticks, or stones for serving and presentation.
4. **Enjoy the Process** : Take your time to prepare, cook, and eat without distractions. Appreciate the sights, smells, and sounds around you.
5. **Eat Mindfully** : Notice how the food tastes different outdoors. Engage all your senses in the experience.

Why This Matters:

- **Develops Survival Skills** : Learning to cook outside is an essential skill for outdoor adventures.
- **Enhances Your Connection with Nature** : The fresh air, natural surroundings, and outdoor cooking create a deeper sensory experience.
- **Encourages Simplicity & Gratitude** : Cooking in nature reminds us how little we actually need to enjoy a meal.

Nature Journal Insight:

- *What did you cook, and how did it turn out?*
- *How was the experience different from cooking indoors?*
- *Did the outdoor setting make your meal feel more enjoyable?*

Day 13: Spotting Wildlife & Understanding Their Role in Ecosystems

Wildlife is all around us, even in urban settings, we just have to slow down and observe. Animals and insects play a crucial role in maintaining ecological balance, and today's challenge is about becoming more aware of their presence and their importance in nature.

How to Do It:

1. **Find a Spot to Observe** : Choose a quiet natural space like a park, forest, lakeside, or even your backyard. Early mornings and evenings are the best times to spot wildlife.
2. **Be Still & Silent** : Animals are more likely to appear when there's minimal human activity. Find a comfortable spot and sit quietly for at least 15:30 minutes.
3. **Look for Signs of Wildlife** : Watch for birds, squirrels, insects, or even signs like footprints, feathers, nests, or burrows.
4. **Use Binoculars or a Camera** : If you have them, use binoculars for a closer look or a camera to capture details.
5. **Research One Species** : Choose one animal or insect you spotted and learn about its habits, diet, and role in the ecosystem.

6. **Record you're Observations** : Write in your nature journal or sketch what you see. Describe their movements, interactions, and surroundings.

Why This Matters:

- **Increases Awareness of Biodiversity** : You'll notice how many creatures coexist with us.
- **Enhances Patience & Observation Skills** : Nature teaches us to slow down and pay attention.
- **Creates a Deeper Connection with Nature** : Understanding wildlife fosters respect and responsibility toward conservation.

Nature Journal Insight:

- *What animals or insects did you observe today?*
- *What did you learn about the species you researched?*
- *Did this experience change the way you see the natural world around you?*

Day 14: Take a Nature Photography Challenge

Photography is a powerful way to capture the beauty of nature and notice details you might otherwise overlook. Today's challenge is all about using your camera or even just your phone to frame the world differently and appreciate the small wonders around you.

How to Do It:

1. **Choose Your Focus** : You can photograph landscapes, wildlife, plants, textures, or even natural patterns like ripples in water or veins in leaves.
2. **Use Natural Lighting** : Try shooting during golden hour, early morning or before sunset for the best natural light.
3. **Experiment with Perspectives** : Take close ups, wide shots, and creative angles to make your photos more interesting.
4. **Capture at Least Five Unique Shots** : Look for different elements, colour, contrast, movement, or hidden details.
5. **Share your favourite Photo** : If you're comfortable, post it on social media or share it with friends with a small caption about why it stood out to you.

Why This Matters:

- **Enhances Observation Skills** : You start noticing beauty in everyday landscapes.
- **Inspires Creativity** : Photography is an artistic way to express your connection with nature.
- **Preserves Memories** : A single photo can bring back the emotions of the moment.

Nature Journal Insight:

- *Which photo was your favourite, and why?*
- *Did this challenge help you see nature from a new perspective?*
- *Will you continue capturing nature through photography in the future?*

Week 3: Disconnect to Reconnect : Finding Inner Peace through Nature

This week is all about slowing down, disconnecting from distractions, and finding inner peace through your connection with nature. After exploring and building outdoor skills, it's time to immerse yourself deeply in the natural world and experience its healing effects.

- You begin with a digital detox day, stepping away from screens to fully embrace the beauty and calmness of nature.
- Practicing outdoor meditation will allow you to cultivate mindfulness, focusing on your breath and surroundings for a deeper sense of relaxation.
- You'll explore the healing power of water by visiting a river, lake, or waterfall, understanding how natural water bodies impact your emotions and well being.

- A day of practicing gratitude in nature will shift your perspective, helping you appreciate the small joys and wonders of the environment.
- You'll develop new awareness by learning to read natural signs, understanding weather patterns, animal behaviours, and plant growth.
- A solo walk in the wilderness will push you to confront solitude, helping you overcome fears and find peace in your own company.
- Finally, you'll experience the magic of sleeping under the stars, immersing yourself in the vastness of the universe and connecting with nature in its purest form.

By the end of Week 3, you'll feel more present, peaceful, and attuned to the rhythms of nature. As you move into Week 4, you'll learn how to make the outdoors a lasting part of your life.

Day 15: A Digital Detox Day : No Screens, Just Nature

In our hyper connected world, we are constantly bombarded with notifications, emails, and endless scrolling. Today's challenge is about stepping away from the digital noise and immersing yourself fully in the real world without screens. By doing so, you'll rediscover the beauty of uninterrupted moments and allow your mind to breathe.

How to Do It:

1. **Commit to a Full Digital Detox** : Turn off your phone, computer, and TV for the entire.
2. **Plan a Nature Focused Activity** : Go for a hike, visit a park, take a long walk, or even just sit under a tree and read a physical book.
3. **Engage with Your Surroundings** : Pay close attention to the colours, textures, and sounds of nature.
4. **Replace Screen Time with Reflection** : Instead of scrolling, write in your journal, meditate, or simply observe the world around you.
5. **Connect with People in Person** : If possible, spend time with family or friends outdoors, engaging in real conversations without digital interruptions.

Why This Matters:

- **Reduces Stress & Mental Overload** : A break from screens improves focus and relaxation.
- **Enhances Mindfulness** : Allows you to be fully present in the moment.
- **Improves Sleep & Mental Clarity** : Less screen exposure, especially in the evening, helps regulate your natural sleep cycle.

Nature Journal Insight:

- *How did it feel to be disconnected from screens for a day?*
- *What did you notice that you usually overlook?*
- *Will you incorporate digital detox days more often?*

Day 16: Meditating Outdoors : Practicing Mindfulness in Natural Surroundings

In the fast paced modern world, our minds are constantly racing filled with endless thoughts, worries, and distractions. Today's challenge is about slowing down, grounding yourself, and embracing mindfulness in nature. Meditating outdoors allows you to find inner peace while connecting deeply with the natural world.

How to Do It:

1. **Choose a Quiet Natural Spot** : Find a peaceful place like a park, forest clearing, riverside, or even your backyard.
2. **Sit Comfortably** : Either cross legged on the ground, on a bench, or lying down if that feels right.
3. **Close Your Eyes & Breathe Deeply** : Take slow, deep breaths in through your nose and out through your mouth.
4. **Focus on Natural Sounds** : Listen to the wind, rustling leaves, birds chirping, or flowing water.
5. **Observe Your Thoughts Without Judgment** : Let your thoughts come and go like passing clouds.
6. **Use a Nature Based Mantra** : Repeat words like *"I am present"* or *"I am connected to nature"* to deepen your focus.

7. **Stay for 10 20 Minutes** : Longer if you wish. Simply be in the moment.

Why This Matters:

- **Reduces Stress & Anxiety** : Deep breathing and mindfulness help lower cortisol levels.
- **Increases Awareness & Presence** : Helps you appreciate the small details of nature.
- **Enhances Mental Clarity** : A calm mind leads to better decision making and creativity.

Nature Journal Insight:

- *How did it feel to meditate in nature compared to indoors?*
- *What sensations, sounds, or thoughts stood out to you?*
- *Will you incorporate outdoor meditation into your routine?*

Day 17: The Healing Power of Water : Visiting a River, Lake, or Waterfall

Water has long been associated with healing, renewal, and tranquillity. From the gentle lapping of waves to the powerful rush of a waterfall, spending time near water can have a deeply calming effect on both the body and mind. Today's challenge is about immersing yourself in the presence of water and experiencing its restorative power.

How to Do It:

1. **Find a Natural Water Source** : Visit a river, lake, pond, waterfall, or even the ocean if possible. If none are nearby, a fountain or garden stream can work too.
2. **Observe the Movement & Sounds** : Sit quietly and watch how the water flows, ripples, or crashes. Listen to the soothing sounds it makes.
3. **Feel the Water** : Dip your hands or feet into the water, feel its temperature, and let its energy refresh you.
4. **Practice Mindful Breathing** : Sync your breaths with the rhythm of the water, inhaling deeply and exhaling slowly.
5. **Connect to it Fully:** If it's safe, take a swim or splash some water on your face to physically connect with its cleansing nature.

Why This Matters:

- **Reduces Stress & Boosts Mental Well Being** : The presence of water naturally soothes the nervous system.
- **Encourages Letting Go** : Watching water move freely can remind us to release our worries.
- **Strengthens Your Connection to Nature** : Helps you appreciate the natural cycles of the earth.

Nature Journal Insight:

- *How did you feel while observing or touching the water?*
- *Did you notice a shift in your emotions or thoughts?*
- *What does water symbolize to you in your life?*

Day 18: Practicing Gratitude in Nature : A Heartfelt Appreciation for the Outdoors

Gratitude is a powerful practice that shifts our perspective from what we lack to what we have. When combined with nature, it becomes even more profound, allowing us to appreciate the beauty, simplicity, and abundance of the natural world. Today's challenge is about slowing down, reflecting, and expressing gratitude for nature and its gifts.

How to Do It:

1. **Find a Peaceful Outdoor Spot** : It could be a park, forest, beach, garden, or even a quiet balcony with greenery.
2. **Take Deep Breaths & Observe Your Surroundings** : Notice the colours, textures, sounds, and scents around you.
3. **Identify Five Things in Nature you're Grateful for** : It could be the warmth of the sun, the cool breeze, the shade of a tree, or the melody of birds.
4. **Express Your Gratitude Out Loud or Silently** : Say "Thank you" to the earth, the sky, or any natural element that resonates with you.
5. **Perform a Small Act of Kindness for Nature** : Pick up litter, water a plant, or feed birds as a token of appreciation.

Why This Matters:

- **Boosts Happiness & Positivity** : Gratitude shifts your focus to life's blessings.
- **Strengthens Your Connection to Nature** : Helps you see yourself as part of the natural world.
- **Encourages Mindful Living** : Being present and appreciative enhances daily experiences.

Nature Journal Insight:

- *What did you feel most grateful for today?*
- *How did expressing gratitude affect your mood?*
- *Will you continue practicing gratitude in nature?*

Day 19: Learning to Read Natural Signs : Weather, Animals, and Plants

Long before modern technology, humans relied on nature's subtle signs to predict weather changes, track animals, and find their way. Today's challenge is about reconnecting with this ancient skill by observing natural patterns in the world around you.

How to Do It:

1. **Observe the Sky & Clouds** : Look at cloud shapes, colours, and movement. Dark, heavy clouds might signal rain, while wispy clouds suggest clear weather.
2. **Listen to Birds & Animal Behaviour** : Birds often quiet down before a storm, and some animals act differently when weather shifts.
3. **Look at Plant Indicators** : Flowers like dandelions and morning glories close up when rain is coming. Some leaves flip upside down in high humidity.
4. **Feel the Wind & Air Pressure** : Sudden temperature drops or shifting winds can indicate an approaching weather change.
5. **Check Tree Rings & Growth Patterns** : If you find a cut tree trunk, look at the rings wider rings mean wet years, while narrow rings indicate drought.

6. **Try Tracking an Animal or Insect** : Look for footprints, broken twigs, or disturbed grass that suggest an animal's recent path.

Why This Matters:

- **Deepens Your Awareness of Nature** : Helps you notice subtle details you may have overlooked.
- **Builds Survival Skills** : Understanding natural signs can be useful in outdoor adventures.
- **Connects You to Ancient Wisdom** : Indigenous cultures and early explorers used these skills for centuries.

Nature Journal Insight:

- *What natural sign surprised you the most?*
- *How do you think learning these skills can help in daily life?*
- *Will you continue practicing reading nature's signals?*

Day 20: A Solo Walk in the Wilderness : Conquering Fear & Finding Solitude

Walking alone in nature can be a transformative experience. It allows you to step away from the noise of daily life, embrace solitude, and build confidence in your ability to navigate the world without distractions. While the idea of a solo walk in the wilderness might feel intimidating at first, today's challenge is about pushing past that fear and embracing the peace that comes with being alone in nature.

How to Do It:

1. **Choose a Safe, Scenic Trail or Path** : Pick a location that you're comfortable with, whether it's a forest trail, a hilltop path, or a quiet lakeside walk.
2. **Leave Your Phone on Silent** : Use it only for emergencies or navigation if needed. The goal is to be truly present.
3. **Walk Slowly & Observe** : Notice the sounds, smells, and sensations of nature. Pay attention to small details like the rustling of leaves or the movement of insects.
4. **Be Alone** : Being alone may feel uncomfortable at first, but try to settle into the quiet and let your thoughts flow freely.

5. **Face Any Fears that Arise** : If you feel uneasy, remind yourself that solitude is a strength, not a weakness.

6. **Reflect Before You Finish** : Find a comfortable spot to sit for a few moments, take deep breaths, and appreciate the solitude.

Why This Matters:

- **Builds Confidence & Self Reliance** : You learn to trust yourself in unfamiliar settings.
- **Reduces Stress & Anxiety** : Solitude in nature has been shown to have calming effects on the mind.
- **Enhances Your Connection with Nature** : Without distractions, you experience nature in its purest form.

Nature Journal Insight:

- *Did you feel uncomfortable being alone in nature? Why or why not?*
- *How did the silence and solitude impact your thoughts?*
- *Would you consider doing more solo nature walks in the future?*

Day 21: Sleeping Under the Stars : The Magic of a Night Outside

There is something deeply magical about sleeping under a vast, starlit sky. It strips away modern comforts and reconnects us to how humans have lived for centuries surrounded by nature, cradled by the sounds of the night. This challenge encourages you to step out of your bedroom and embrace the experience of a night under the stars, whether in your backyard, a campsite, or a remote wilderness spot.

How to Do It:

1. **Choose Your Sleeping Spot** : If you're new to sleeping outdoors, your backyard or a safe, nearby location is a great start. If you're comfortable, try a quiet camping area or an open field.
2. **Bring the Essentials** : A sleeping bag, mat, or even just a blanket will keep you comfortable. Dress in layers to stay warm.
3. **Go Tech Free** : Minimize phone use to fully immerse yourself in the natural experience.
4. **Observe the Night Sky** : Before sleeping, take time to gaze at the stars. Try identifying constellations or simply admire the vastness above.

5. **Listen to Nature** : The sounds of nocturnal creatures, rustling leaves, and the whispering wind create a natural lullaby.
6. **Let Yourself Relax** : Embrace the feeling of being a small part of the universe. Let go of any fears and allow yourself to feel safe in nature's embrace.

Why This Matters:

- **Boosts a Sense of Adventure** : Sleeping outdoors can feel thrilling and liberating.
- **Improves Sleep Quality** : Exposure to fresh air and natural darkness supports better sleep.
- **Strengthens Your Connection to the Universe** : Looking at the stars reminds us of how vast and wondrous the world truly is.

Nature Journal Insight:

- *How did it feel to sleep without walls around you?*
- *Did you notice any thoughts or emotions arise during the night?*
- *Would you do it again? Why or why not?*

Week 4: Living the Outdoor Lifestyle : Making Nature a Part of You

As you step into the final week of this challenge, the focus shifts from short term experiences to **embracing nature as a lifelong lifestyle**. This week is about applying everything you've learned and committing to an outdoor friendly mindset.

- You'll begin by **planning a multi day camping trip**, giving you a full experience of outdoor living and self sufficiency.
- **Foraging and identifying edible plants** will introduce you to sustainable ways of gathering food from nature.
- A deep dive into **sustainable outdoor living** will teach you the principles of "Leave No Trace" ethics, ensuring that you enjoy nature responsibly.
- Giving back to nature is essential, so you'll spend a day **volunteering for a conservation project** to help protect the environment.

- **Building a survival kit** will prepare you for future adventures, equipping you with essential tools and knowledge for safety in the wild.
- To make this journey personal, you'll **write your own nature manifesto**, defining what nature means to you and how you plan to keep it part of your life.
- **Sharing your experiences** will inspire others to embark on their own journey with nature, creating a ripple effect of outdoor enthusiasm.
- A **reflective walk** will help you look back on your progress, appreciating your growth and the changes this challenge has brought.
- Finally, in the **ultimate challenge**, you'll commit to integrating nature into your daily life, ensuring that this journey doesn't end here, it becomes a way of living.

Week 4 is about transformation. By the time you finish this challenge, nature will no longer be something you visit, it will be a part of who you are.

Day 22: Planning a Multi Day Camping Trip : Taking the Next Big Step

After three weeks of immersing yourself in nature through small but meaningful activities, it's time to take things up a notch. A multi day camping trip is an adventure that will push your limits, teach you self sufficiency, and deepen your connection with the natural world. Whether you go solo or with friends, this experience will be a turning point in your journey to making the outdoors a way of life.

How to Do It:

1. **Choose Your Destination** : Pick glamping sites or raw campsites, near national park, forest, river or mountains. Research trails, water sources, and camping regulations.
2. **Plan Your Essentials** : Make a checklist of what you need, this time choose a fully included camping site:
    - First aid kit
    - Navigation tools (map, compass, GPS)
    - Proper clothing and layers
    - Light source (headlamp or flashlight)
3. **Prepare for the Unexpected** : Learn basic survival skills, such as fire starting, filtering water, and handling wildlife encounters.
4. **Set a Goal for the Trip** : Will this be a time for self reflection, physical challenge, or simply

unwinding in nature? Having a purpose will make the experience more meaningful.

5. **Go Off Grid** : Limit phone use, embrace solitude, and fully experience the sights, sounds, and energy of nature.
6. **Leave No Trace** : Be responsible with waste, respect wildlife, and ensure not to throw waste on your trails or outside campsite.

Why This Matters:

- **Builds Self Sufficiency** : You'll learn how to rely on your skills, instincts, and preparation.
- **Develops a Stronger Connection with Nature** : Spending multiple days outside allows you to fully sync with the natural world.
- **Boosts Confidence & Resilience** : Overcoming minor challenges in the wild prepares you for bigger challenges in life.

Nature Journal Insight:

- *What part of the planning process excited or intimidated you the most?*
- *How do you feel about spending multiple days outdoors?*
- *What are you most looking forward to on your camping trip?*

Day 23: Foraging & Understanding Edible Wild Plants : A Taste of the Wild

Foraging is one of the oldest survival skills, allowing us to connect deeply with nature by understanding what it offers as nourishment. Learning about edible wild plants not only enhances outdoor skills but also fosters a greater appreciation for the ecosystem. Knowing how to identify, harvest, and use wild plants safely can be both a fun and empowering experience.

How to Do It:

1. **Do Your Research First** : Read a beginner's guide to wild foraging. Learn to distinguish between edible and poisonous plants. Understand ethical foraging practices, never overharvest and leave enough for wildlife.
2. **Start with the Basics** : Look for easily identifiable edible plants, such as dandelions, wild berries, or clover. Avoid plants growing near roadsides or polluted areas. If in doubt, **do not eat it!** Use field guides or apps to verify plant safety.
3. **Try a Simple Recipe** : Brew herbal tea using wild mint or chamomile. Make a wild greens salad with dandelion leaves, clover, and plantain leaves. Try roasting nuts or seeds found in the wild.

Why This Matters:

- **Survival Skill** : In remote areas, knowing how to identify edible plants can be life saving.
- **Health Benefits** : Many wild plants are nutrient dense and free from pesticides.
- **Deeper Connection to Nature** : Foraging makes you more mindful of seasonal changes and plant ecosystems.

Nature Journal Insight:

- *What plants did you discover today? Were any of them edible?*
- *How did foraging change the way you see the natural world?*
- *Would you consider incorporating wild foods into your diet more often?*

Day 24: Sustainable Outdoor Living : Leaving No Trace

Nature gives us so much peace, adventure, and a place to reconnect with ourselves. In return, we have a responsibility to protect it. **"Leave No Trace" (LNT)** is an essential philosophy for outdoor enthusiasts, ensuring that we enjoy nature **without harming it.** Today's challenge is about learning and practicing **sustainable outdoor living** so that future generations can experience the same beauty.

How to Do It:

1. **Plan Smart:** Research your destination, pack eco friendly essentials, and bring reusable items to reduce waste.
2. **Stick to the Trails:** Avoid damaging fragile plants by staying on designated paths and campsites.
3. **Pack It In, Pack It Out:** Carry all trash back with you even if it's not yours. Leave nature cleaner than you found it.
4. **Respect Wildlife:** Observe from a distance, never feed animals, and store food properly to avoid disturbing ecosystems.
5. **Minimize Campfire Impact:** Use a stove for cooking instead of making fires. If fires are allowed, keep them small and fully extinguish them.

6. **Leave What You Find:** Admire rocks, plants, and artifacts where they belong take only pictures, leave only footprints.

Why This Matters:

- Preserves the natural environment for future explorers.
- Prevents pollution and protects wildlife.
- Teaches mindfulness and respect for the outdoors.

Nature Journal Insight:

- *Did today's challenge change the way you see your impact on nature?*
- *What's one thing you can commit to doing differently in your outdoor adventures?*
- *How did it feel to leave a place exactly as you found it or even cleaner?*

Day 25: Volunteering for a Nature Conservation Project : Giving Back to the Outdoors

Spending time in nature gives us a sense of peace, adventure, and freedom. But it's also important to **give back** to the natural world that provides us with so much. Today's challenge is about **taking action** whether by volunteering for a conservation project, participating in a clean up, or supporting an environmental cause. Even small contributions make a **huge impact** in protecting and restoring nature.

How to Do It:

1. **Find a Local Project** : Look for conservation groups or national parks that offer volunteer opportunities. Many have programs for tree planting, clean ups, and wildlife protection.
2. **Join a Clean up Drive** : Participate in a beach, forest, or trail clean up. Even picking up litter during your hikes makes a difference!
3. **Help with Reforestation** : Volunteer to plant trees or restore damaged ecosystems. Every tree planted helps combat deforestation and climate change.
4. **Support Wildlife Conservation** : Assist in animal rescue, habitat restoration, or awareness programs. Some organizations let you adopt or sponsor an animal.

5. **Educate & Inspire Others** : Spread awareness about nature conservation. Share your experience, teach kids about protecting the environment, or organize an awareness event.
6. **Make It a Habit** : Volunteering doesn't have to be a one time activity. Find small ways to contribute regularly, like donating to environmental causes or reducing your ecological footprint.

Why This Matters:

- **Protects natural spaces** for future generations.
- **Restores balance** in fragile ecosystems.
- **Helps wildlife thrive** in cleaner, healthier environments.
- **Creates a sense of purpose** and deeper connection to nature.

Nature Journal Insight:

- *How did today's challenge make you feel?*
- *What kind of conservation work would you like to do more often?*
- *Did this experience change the way you see your responsibility toward nature?*

Day 26: Building a Survival Kit for Future Adventures : Be Ready for Anything

Being outdoors is a thrilling experience, but nature is unpredictable. Whether you're heading on a short hike or a multi day camping trip, having a well prepared **survival kit** can make the difference between a smooth adventure and a risky situation. Today's challenge is all about **building your own essential survival kit** something that will keep you safe, comfortable, and ready for future adventures.

How to Do It:

1. **Choose the Right Backpack** : Pick a lightweight, durable bag to store your survival essentials without weighing you down.
2. **Pack the Basics** : Always carry a first aid kit, multi tool, flashlight, extra batteries, and waterproof matches or a lighter.
3. **Stay Hydrated & Nourished** : Include a reusable water bottle, water purification tablets, and energy packed snacks like nuts and protein bars.
4. **Prepare for Emergencies** : Keep an emergency whistle, a signal mirror, and a compact survival blanket for unexpected situations.
5. **Navigation is Key** : Bring a map, compass, or GPS device to avoid getting lost in unfamiliar terrain.
6. **Personalize Your Kit** : Adapt your survival kit based on your adventure type whether it's hiking, camping, or extreme weather conditions.

Why This Matters:

- **Boosts confidence & preparedness** for any outdoor challenge.
- **Ensures safety** in case of unexpected weather or emergencies.
- **Encourages self sufficiency** and resourcefulness in nature.
- **Could save your life** in extreme situations!

Nature Journal Insight:

- *Did you already have some survival gear, or did you need to build your kit from scratch?*
- *What was the most important item you packed?*
- *Do you feel more prepared for future adventures now?*

Day 27: Writing Your Own Nature Manifesto : Defining Your Relationship with the Wild

By now, you've spent nearly a month reconnecting with nature watching sunrises, hiking trails, learning survival skills, and finding peace in the great outdoors. **But what does all of this mean for you moving forward?** Today's challenge is about reflecting on your journey and writing your own **Nature Manifesto** a personal declaration of how you want to live in harmony with nature from this day on.

How to Do It:

1. **Reflect on Your Experiences** : Think about what nature means to you and how it has impacted your life so far.
2. **Define Your Core Values** : Identify key principles like respect, sustainability, and adventure that will guide your outdoor lifestyle.
3. **Write in Your Own Words** : Your manifesto should be personal and inspiring keep it simple, honest, and from the heart.
4. **Set Intentions for the Future** : Outline how you will stay connected with nature, whether through regular hikes, conservation efforts, or mindful outdoor practices.
5. **Make It Visible** : Write it in your journal, frame it, or keep it somewhere you'll see it often as a reminder of your commitment.

6. **Share & Inspire** : Encourage others to create their own nature manifesto and start living in harmony with the wild.

Example Manifesto:

"I will seek adventure in the wild and embrace the unknown. I will protect nature as it has protected me. I will walk barefoot on the earth, listen to the whispers of the trees, and breathe in the fresh air deeply. I will explore with curiosity, respect every creature, and leave no trace behind. I will not let screens and city noise take away my connection to the land. Nature is my refuge, my teacher, and my home. I belong to the wild."

Feel free to get creative! Write it as a poem, a letter to yourself, or a pledge.

Why This Matters:

- **Defines your long term commitment** to nature.
- **Deepens your connection** with the outdoors.
- **Helps you stay grounded** even when life gets busy.
- **Encourages eco conscious decisions** in everyday life.

Nature Journal Insight:

- *How do you want to live in harmony with nature?*
- *What changes will you make in your daily life to stay connected to the outdoors?*
- *If you could give one message to future generations about nature, what would it be?*

Day 28: Sharing Your Experiences : Inspiring Others to Join the Challenge

You've nearly completed this 30 day journey what an incredible achievement! Over the past few weeks, you've stepped outside your comfort zone, embraced the wilderness, and formed a deeper connection with nature. But your adventure doesn't have to end here.

Today's challenge is about **spreading the message and inspiring others to reconnect with nature** through your own experiences. By sharing your story, you can ignite a spark in someone else and encourage them to embark on their own outdoor adventure.

How to Do It:

1. **Tell Your Story** : Share your outdoor journey through blogs, social media, or simple conversations with friends and family.
2. **Use Photos & Videos** : A picture speaks a thousand words capture, your experiences to inspire others visually.
3. **Encourage Participation** : Invite friends to join you on a hike, camping trip, or even a small nature challenge.
4. **Educate & Motivate** : Share tips, lessons, and sustainable practices you've learned to help others connect with nature.
5. **Create a Community** : Start a nature loving group, online or offline, where people can share their adventures and learn from each other.

6. **Lead by Example** : Live the outdoor lifestyle every day and show others the joy and peace that nature can bring.

Why This Matters:

- **Inspires others** to reconnect with the outdoors.
- **Spreads awareness** about the benefits of nature.
- **Keeps your passion alive** by sharing and reliving your experience.

Nature Journal Insight:

- *Who do you want to inspire with your story?*
- *How can you continue to bring nature into your daily life?*
- *What advice would you give to someone hesitant about spending time outdoors?*

Day 29: A Reflective Walk : Revisiting Your Journey & Growth

You've come so far on this journey of deepening your connection with nature, pushing past personal boundaries, and embracing the beauty of the world around you. Today, before we reach the final day, it's time to **slow down, reflect, and truly absorb everything you've experienced**.

This challenge is about **taking a walk down memory lane both physically and mentally**. You'll revisit a place you've explored during this journey, reflect on your growth, and acknowledge the changes in your mindset and spirit.

How to Do It:

1. **Take a Solo Walk** : Choose a peaceful trail or park and walk without distractions, focusing on your journey so far.
2. **Reflect on Your Growth** : Think about how your mindset, habits, and connection with nature have evolved.
3. **Revisit favourite Spots** : Walk through places that had a special impact on you during this challenge and recall those moments.
4. **Express Gratitude** : Appreciate the lessons learned, the beauty of nature, and the personal growth you've achieved.

5. **Journal Your Thoughts** : Write down your reflections, emotions, and key takeaways from the experience.
6. **Plan for the Future** : Set intentions on how you will continue to integrate nature into your daily life.

Why This Matters:

- Helps **you recognize** how far you've come.
- Creates a **moment of gratitude** for the journey.
- Reinforces **your commitment** to an outdoor lifestyle.
- Provides **clarity on your next steps** after the challenge.

Nature Journal Insight:

- *If you could go back to **Day 1**, what would you tell yourself?*
- *What part of this challenge will you carry forward into your daily life?*
- *How will you inspire others to connect with nature?*

Day 30: The Final Challenge : Committing to a Life with Nature

You made it! **30 days of exploring, learning, and growing with nature.** What started as a simple challenge has now transformed into a way of life. Today is not the end it's a new beginning. The real challenge now is **keeping this connection alive beyond these 30 days** and integrating nature into your daily routine.

This final day is about **celebrating your journey, recognizing your transformation, and making a lifelong commitment to the natural world**.

How to Do It:

1. **Make a Personal Pledge** : Write down a commitment to keep nature a part of your life, whether through regular hikes, outdoor mindfulness, or sustainable living.
2. **Create a Nature Routine** : Schedule weekly or monthly outdoor activities to maintain your connection with nature.
3. **Inspire Others** : Share your experience with friends and family, encouraging them to explore and appreciate the outdoors.
4. **Set a Long Term Goal** : Plan a future adventure, like a multi day trek or conservation volunteering, to keep your outdoor spirit alive.
5. **Continue Learning** : Read books, watch documentaries, or join outdoor communities to deepen your knowledge and love for nature.

6. **Stay Mindful & Grateful** : Carry the lessons from this journey forward, appreciating every sunrise, trail, and moment of peace in the wild.

Why This Matters:

- **You've built a deep bond with nature** now it's time to nurture it.
- **Turning a challenge into a lifestyle** is the key to lasting change.
- **Your commitment today** will influence how you live in the years to come.

Nature Journal Insight:

- How has this journey changed your perspective on life?
- What lessons from nature will you carry forward?
- How will you encourage others to embrace the outdoors?

Lessons from the Wild

This is not the end it's just the beginning of your lifelong adventure with nature. Whether it's a simple walk in the park or a grand expedition into the wild, always remember **the peace, wisdom, and joy that nature brings**.

Thank you for taking on this challenge. **You've officially escaped the ordinary.** Now, go and live a life connected to the wild!

A New Beginning

How This Challenge Changed You?

As you stand at the end of this 30 day journey, take a deep breath and look back at where you started. What began as a simple challenge has now transformed into something much greater, an awakening, a shift in perspective, and a deeper connection with the natural world.

Through each step, whether it was waking up with the sunrise, walking barefoot on the earth, or spending a night under the stars, you have slowly unshackled yourself from the fast paced, screen driven life and stepped into a world of presence, simplicity, and adventure.

You've discovered that nature isn't just a place to visit it's a part of you. The trees you walked past, the rivers you listened to, and the fresh air you breathed have become more than just elements of the environment; they are now familiar friends, silent teachers, and eternal reminders of what it means to truly live.

But most importantly, you have changed. You've grown in ways you may not have even realized yet. Your patience has deepened, your appreciation for small moments has expanded, and your ability to find joy in simplicity has strengthened. You have reconnected not just with nature, but with yourself.

As this challenge comes to an end, a new question arises: **What comes next?**

The Next Steps : Turning This into a Lifelong Habit

Completing a **30 day challenge** is a remarkable achievement, but the true transformation begins when you integrate these experiences into your everyday life. Nature is not meant to be a one time escape it's a lifelong companion, a constant source of inspiration, peace, and adventure.

The key to making this journey last is **intentionality**. Now that you've spent a month rediscovering the great outdoors, ask yourself: **How can I make this a part of my routine?**

1. Create a Weekly Nature Ritual

You don't have to spend hours every day in the wild, but a small weekly habit can keep you connected. It could be:

- A morning walk in the park every Sunday.
- A solo hike or camping trip once a month.
- Watching the sunrise or stargazing at least once a week.
- Setting aside time to sit in silence by a lake or river.

Find what resonates with you and commit to it.

2. Stay Curious & Keep Learning

Nature has endless lessons to teach. Keep exploring, discovering, and learning. Some ways to do this are:

- Reading books about wilderness survival, outdoor skills, or conservation.
- Learning to identify local birds, plants, and weather patterns.
- Watching documentaries about nature and the environment.
- Trying new outdoor hobbies like kayaking, rock climbing, or foraging.

Every new skill or experience deepens your connection to the natural world.

3. Reduce Digital Dependence & Live More Mindfully

One of the biggest takeaways from this challenge is learning to be present. The modern world constantly pulls us into distractions, but nature reminds us to slow down.

- Set technology free hours in your day to disconnect.
- Practice mindfulness, observe the small details around you.
- Prioritize outdoor activities over screen time.

Your ability to disconnect from distractions is what allows you to truly reconnect with nature and yourself.

4. Share Your Journey & Inspire Others

One of the most powerful ways to keep yourself accountable is to share your journey with others.

- Invite friends or family to join you on hikes or camping trips.
- Write about your experiences in a blog or journal.
- Share nature photography or reflections on social media.
- Teach kids or younger generations about the importance of the outdoors.

By inspiring others, you also strengthen your own commitment.

5. Support & Protect Nature

Nature has given you so much peace, adventure, clarity, and joy. Now, it's time to give back.

- Support conservation efforts in your area.
- Participate in clean up drives or tree planting initiatives.
- Be mindful of your environmental footprint reduce waste, recycle, and choose sustainable travel options.

Nature thrives when we care for it, and in return, it continues to nurture us.

Lessons from the Wild

This 30 day challenge was just the beginning. Every moment you spent outdoors watching the sunrise, feeling the earth beneath your feet, or sleeping under the stars was a step toward something greater. **A life filled with adventure, peace, and a deep connection with the natural world.**

The journey never truly ends, it simply evolves. So, step outside, take a deep breath, and keep walking this path. **Nature will always be there, waiting for you.**

Journaling Prompts for Self Reflection

Journaling is a powerful way to deepen your connection with nature and reflect on your personal growth throughout your outdoor experiences. Use these prompts to capture your thoughts, emotions, and lessons learned during your journey.

Connecting with Nature

- What is your favourite place in nature, and why does it feel special to you?
- Describe a moment in nature that made you feel completely at peace.
- How has your perception of nature changed since you started spending more time outdoors?
- If you could immerse yourself in any natural landscape for a week, where would it be and why?
- Write about a time when nature helped you overcome stress or a personal challenge.

Personal Growth & Adventure

- What fears or challenges have you faced in the outdoors, and how did you overcome them?
- How has this experience helped you build confidence and resilience?
- What outdoor activity pushed you out of your comfort zone the most? How did you feel afterward?

- If you could give your past self one piece of advice before starting this journey, what would it be?
- Describe a moment of joy, awe, or wonder you experienced in nature.

Mindfulness & Gratitude

- What are five things in nature that you're grateful for?
- How does being in nature influence your mood and mindset?
- Reflect on a time when you felt truly present in the moment while outdoors.
- What lessons has nature taught you about patience, resilience, or simplicity?
- How can you bring more mindfulness into your daily outdoor experiences?

Living in Harmony with Nature

- How has this journey influenced your attitude toward environmental conservation?
- What small changes can you make in your daily life to live more sustainably?
- How do you feel about the idea of leaving no trace in nature? Have your habits changed?
- Describe how you can inspire others to connect with and protect the natural world.
- What commitment will you make to continue exploring and respecting nature in the future?

A Note of Gratitude

Writing this book has been a journey of growth, discovery, and deep connection with nature, and I couldn't have done it alone.

To my readers Thank you for embarking on this adventure with me. Whether you've followed each challenge step by step or taken small moments to reconnect with nature, I hope this book has inspired you to see the world with fresh eyes. Your willingness to embrace the outdoors, step out of your comfort zone, and find peace in nature means more than words can express.

To my family and loved ones your unwavering support, patience, and encouragement have been my greatest source of strength. Thank you for believing in me, for cheering me on, and for understanding my passion for the wild.

To the natural world itself thank you for being my greatest teacher. The forests, rivers, mountains, and open skies have offered lessons no book alone could teach.

This is not the end but a new beginning. Keep exploring, keep learning, and most importantly, keep embracing the beauty of the world around you.

With gratitude,
Aditya Ruhela

www.ingramcontent.com/pod-product-compliance
Lightning Source LLC
Chambersburg PA
CBHW062111160726
48282CB00026B/759

* 9 7 8 9 3 3 4 2 7 7 0 8 1 *